AWAKENED BY THE LIGHT

SABINA ZAK

Printed in the United States of America

Designed by Chelcey Farrar of C. Farrar Designs

ISBN 9798526782265

I am who I am
At least I think I know
I'm tough on the outside
And within my core

Decisions I've made long ago
Cultivated my soul
Because I had to grow
And be on my own

Alone I have raised two beautiful beings
I gave them my whole
Because of my goal
For them to feel complete

Alone is a long curvy road
With repeating rotundas
And messages to encode
A journey to love and to endure

But now I am ready to see beyond
Awakened by the light
With so much delight
Life is not just black and white

The fork of opportunities
Can be difficult to see
Especially when the fork
Is not visible initially

Life's journey must be redirected
For ultimate fulfillment to be achieved
This may not always be pleasant
And sometimes even hurt your essence

What happiness is depends on you
Others' business not relevant to you
Their happiness won't rob you
Of what is meant for you

The path of our journey
Is not always easy
It can be treacherous at times
But always very revealing

People can be ruthless unkind and vengeful
Their uttered words can be disrespectful
Hurtful to others and often painful
Think before you speak and be careful

The negative energy set abound
Will be redirected to that one
The one with ugly words uttered
Will be the one most negatively bothered

To others I say what I say to myself
Be proactive and not reactive
Practice affection and reflection
Because rejection is redirection

I'm tough on the outside and within my core

ROSE

I see you sitting right
There in front of me
With heavy shoulders
Waiting patiently to be free

I see you sitting there
Across the wooden table
Sipping bottled club soda
Tied down by a thick cable

We talk about life and the little things too
Every time you smile I feel that you do
Need to shrug off that burden deep inside
Buried and hidden within you

The message for you is very clear
I said it because you are very dear
A Friendship that began years ago
Will continue to flourish and grow even more

The YOU inside yearning to come out
Silently screaming "let me out"
You don't see it, but I do
A better life is waiting for you

To get there you need to face the truth
Understand your fears and feelings too
Be honest with yourself and accept that its fine
To love yourself like fine wine

The men in your life provided you with comfort
Their love was so reassuring
And when they left you
It was so disturbing

Instead you smiled and said "all is okay "
You kept your emotions at bay
Strong women don't cry you say
They keep on going and continue to pray

Years passed on and now we are here
Your mounted feelings continue to be
A source of your weakness and fears
Bringing you down to your knees

You are ready now to face the truth
To see beyond and deep into your soul
To free yourself from hurtful past
And to know you are free at last

You don't see it, but I do
A better life is waiting for you

NAVUSH

How fabulous it is to know
The secrets of this universe
Unveil themselves and unfold
Finally embedded and immersed

Situations arise and display
Repeat themselves nonetheless
For humankind to overcome
The wisdom in it embraced

Reactions often overstated
Displeasures manifested
Lacking knowledge of the truth
Reality becomes undigested

The differences you see
Depends on what you think
Consciousness is awareness
Kool-aid for you to drink

Dive deep into thought
Negative impressions fought
Enlighten the moments presented
Emerged energy sought

How beautiful it is
To own the tools you need
The universe will work your way
A magnificent life to awaiting through the archway

How beautiful it is
to own the tools you need

SECRETS

I am destined to be me

Years passed by
And I am much older
I wish that I could
Look over my shoulder

It is what it is
A man inapt
A victim I am
I have to adapt

The time is right
To say goodbye
To this old life
I will Not cry

Tears that shed
Dried up by now
It's time to move on
Time to pow-wow

Strong and resilient
Is who I am
I don't need you
As a man

I am a woman
Independent and free
I am
Destined to be me

RISE UP NATALIE

I often ponder
Where it all went wrong
Life isn't fitting
Like a bad pair of thongs

The promises made
Fulfilled they were not
Cruel words were spoken
Like a noose with a tight knot

Perseverance and pursuit
To continue to wound
My bleeding heart
Remained attuned

To love and to hold
To always be together
In good and in bad
Rough like reptile leather

Longing to be caressed
Loved and appreciated
The intentions you set
Kept me neglected

The pain is real
But the hole is deeper
Darkness inside
Will it ever be clearer

There's no way out
Out of this miserable mind
Except to surrender
I need peace to find

The tree of life
Is also my only way out
I get that thick rope
I know this without any doubt

So off I go without hesitation
To a better world I hope
Unbound unconfined
Without any pressure

The tree now harboring my secrets
Absorbing my salty tears
Hiding my screams and
Holding me by a long string

What has happened
For me to feel this way
I've sunken deeper
In big dismay

I look out the window
I see a tree of life
It gives me hope
So I can be good to my wife

I spin in darkness
With no light in sight
The curtains are closing
It's not even dark outside

No one can help me
I'm too far gone
The thoughts of misery
Sad feelings that can't be undone

The pain is real
It really hurts
No where to escape
I'm very lost

GUY

Nowhere to escape

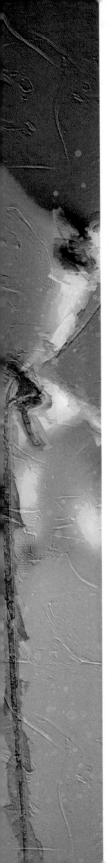

Today is your birthday
Its that time again
To send you warm wishes
With so much zen

To say that you're special
Is really not fair
You are so much more
A love affair

Your presence
Is real
A glimpse of the light
Its so right

The Magic lives on
Because of your love
A destiny manifested
A plan requested

I wish you the best
Like I always do
While awake and asleep
I am grateful for you

Happy birthday to you
A feeling so deep
May you always be healthy
With crops to reap

*I wish you the best
like I always do*

HAPPY BIRTHDAY

The smell of the ocean
Sunset sky
An overwhelming feeling
That just can't be denied

The energy is flowing
A picture emerging
A grandiose door
An opportunity lurking

Intuitions so strong
Knowing what's coming
Accepting the truth
Is the way of becoming

Challenging moments
Ego at bay
Not succumbing
To emotions and despair

Knowing your worth
Needless to say
Is more important
Than being a prey

Accepting change
Is a marvelous feeling
The universe's way
Of a new beginning

Accepting the truth
is the way of becoming

REFLECTION

Ain't it great
When our souls have met
Destined to cross paths
A relationship to last

Your voice caught my attention
Mesmerized by the sound
My body vibrated
It was so profound

It was instant connection
Organized from above
A promise I made
Long ago - before this life

Words never spoken
Don't need to be
Messages communicated
Though wavelength frequency

Bound by your presence
Admiration and love
A match made in heaven
Like a hand in a glove

Feelings of comfort
So naturally flowing
How I want it to be
Forever glowing

I miss you each day
When you are not near
Desiring to be
In your premier

Whatever may be
I know it for sure
A fairytale story
Emerging on its own

Desiring to be in your premier

TWO SOULS

Chaos frustration
Around us is clear
The stars in retrograde
It's time to be free

Manage organize oversee
For reasons unknown
Reactions overblown
It's hard to see

Patience a virtue
How long will it last
Mind is screaming
Free me alas

Drama compounding
Stress level high
Honestly people
Chill out and just smile

Egos dominance
Control is the game
Tame others slowly
Power to be gained

I smile and say
Next phase is near
For new beginnings
A happy new year

KARMA

TABLE OF CONTENTS

I am often reminded that our connections to one another are immersed in meaning and as humans we enjoy forging connections with the unique people who come into our lives. Philosophically, the theory of six degrees of separation, a connectivity constant for humanity, reiterates that rather than being separated we are all connected. Some connections will be immediate and lifelong. Some will be short lived but the lessons will be learned. Everyone has the ability to make a difference and everything happens for a reason. Throughout, Love is the glue that binds us all together.

We all face various difficulties to some extent and everyday challenges are a natural phenomenon along this journey of life. Our collective reactions to obstacles influence much of the outcome we experience physically, emotionally, mentally and spiritually. The choices are ours to make and the fork of opportunities lie ahead. To make better choices for improved vitality, we must first be "awakened by the light." We must be aware of our conscious and subconscious states of being. In my own journey of awakening, I have been blessed to be intuned to my inner self and to others' journeys and their unique challenges. Their stories and mine are told in this poem book. The poems are real depictions of a soul's life struggles and their deep inner feelings.

I encourage you all to be awakened and aware. We are the authors of our stories.

Let the light shine bright and continue to illuminate us all.

- Sabina Zak

She came like a spirit so gentle

like a hovering angel

Thank you to all of you who inspire me along my journey. The light you shine is always appreciated.

Special thank you to Dr. Oded Preis for writing such a heartfelt and humbling poem. It truly touches my soul. The simple things we do often have the greatest impact..

She came to me in moment of desperation
Painful loss and separation
She came like a spirit so gentle
Like a hovering angel
Scent so intoxicating and sweet
From pain an instant retreat
Words of kindness follow
Like a drug extricating sorrow
Eyes with tears swell
Draw you in like an infinite well
Warm and gentle soul
Achy spirit console
Warm gentle caress and embrace
Relieves torture and stress

By Oded Preis MD

Time
A blink of an eye
A new picture emerges
to only pass by

Time passes by and
with each ticking day

Time

Oh! What a sight
To see the morning sunlight
Arising shyly at dawn
Bringing bright light into the world

The reflections of rays
Onto endless water bays
Comforting my soul
Deep into my core

The glistening shimmering light
Glowing silently while it's still quite dark
The energy is confounding
At the same time so relaxing

I'm reminded of true essence
Re-tuning my reflections
The purpose in this life
To guide others in their lives

Comforting my soul,
deep into my core

Sunlight

Boo-boom boo-boom and so it goes
My heart palpates and thumps across
Across my chest it beats so fast
How long will it last

My breath is heavy it is hard to breathe
My hands shake and feel weak
The burning sensation continues to be
And I don't feel like this is me

Thoughts erratic and all over the place
My mind races and as I look at my face
Uneasy and nervous my being is
All I want to do is scream

I Scream out loud but no sound comes out
I explode to pieces and shatter throughout
Broken I feel as I weep
Help me help me I just want to sleep

Hope to pick up the pieces to help me be
Without any stress nor chaos within me
The turmoil will leave me one day
When perhaps you look my way

*ss my chest it beats sof
how long will it last*

*I see you exist,
inside and out*

I SEE YOU EXIST

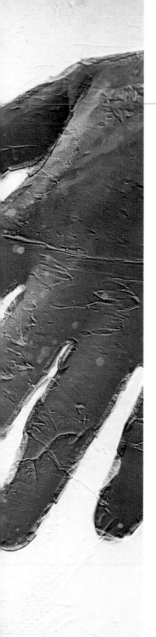

I see you exist
Inside and out
Confused and lost
Without a shadow of a doubt

I lend out my hand
Without you shaking it back
I hurt for your status
And give you feedback

You turn away
Cause you can't face the facts
You pretend it doesn't exist
And then you retract

The hole is getting deeper
And you feel there's no way out
Compounded by deep emotions
You cry on the inside

Pretending all is OK
Is your way to exist
Otherwise you will sink
Deeper into the abyss

You know you can
And one day you will
Awaken and aware
You will go uphill

I'm here for you now
Tomorrow and after
Support you somehow
To hear your laughter

I hope that you will
Open up and hear
The message is here
You only need to persevere

*I wither away,
like a rotten flower*

RAVISHED

I stay still as
I lay there quietly
I close my eyes
Innocent and young

I cringe deep inside
Knowing what's to come
Body shaken
No where to run

The moment is here
Why would it be me
I hope and pray
To be over and be free

Scared and in pain
Will it ever end
My body is melting
As I transcend

I wither away
Like a rotten flower
Breath goes away
I don't matter

You care from afar
sending your love

FRIDAY NIGHT

It's Friday night
Shabbat is here
We lit up the candles
And did our routine

This time my prayer
Ended with an ask
For you to come back
So it won't be dark

You can't be here
Because you are there
I know you are peaceful
And that you care

You care from afar
Sending your love
Talking to me
All from above

When I'm deep in thoughts
You make sure to say
Say what you want
In your own way

Thank you for being
The person you are
In spirit and soul
You are my all-star

This journey is all yours
a life complete and full of growth

WATERFALL IN THE DESERT

At time of despair
I look up and you are there
Looking at me from up above
Sending kisses with tremendous love

Life can be sometimes hard
Struggles inflicted not always bad
Loneliness ensues and you feel sad
Emptiness inside like dunes of sand

You make a choice you see
To sink or float above the sea
Mind body and soul connected
A waterfall in the desert

A legacy of life imprinted
The voyage is somewhat prescriptive
This journey is all yours
A life complete and full of growth

Your beating heart,

as one with mine

SOUL MATE

How long has it been love
Since our eyes met in person
How long has it been love
Since your lips tasted mine

Missing your warm touch
Our fingers intertwined
Your beating heart
As one with mine

The butterflies are tickling
And dancing around
In my belly that is
Just thinking of you abound

Imagine the time
Of our reunion to be
A spark of heaven will be
Shining forever in what feels like

Eternity

WE ARE COLOR

We are here for each other
Beyond and Above

We are color
The color of love
Masked on the outside
Same on the inside

We are people
With different backgrounds
Brought up in silos
Forget to love

Love is all that matters
Believe it or not
You pave the wave
For a better future to come

Knots can be untangled
If we choose it to be
We forget that we can
Freedom is real

Remember what matters
The little things in life
We are here for each other
Beyond and above

THE GIRL IN THE MIRROR

I look in the mirror
And what I see
Is a picture of someone
Who isn't me

I look in the mirror
And see a face
Unique and afraid
With so much grace

The laughter masked by fake
Smiles that No one can see
On phony Snapchat
My spirit yearning to be free

Anxiety compounding
Fast beating heart
My palms are sweaty
But I play the part

*I look in the mirror
and see a face*

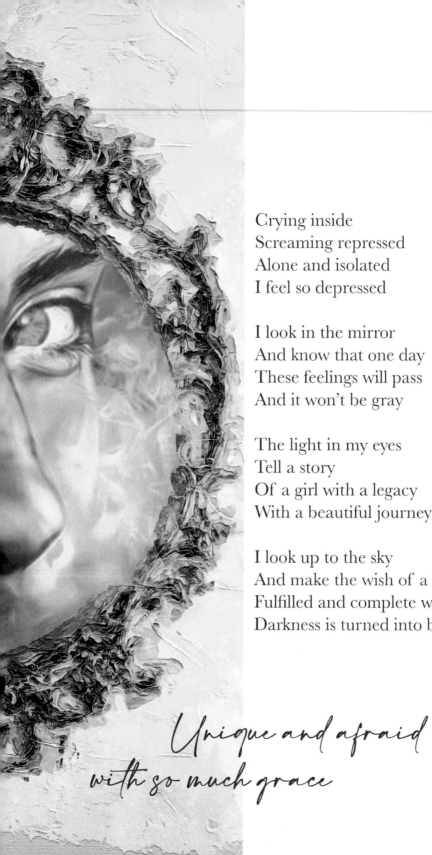

Crying inside
Screaming repressed
Alone and isolated
I feel so depressed

I look in the mirror
And know that one day
These feelings will pass
And it won't be gray

The light in my eyes
Tell a story
Of a girl with a legacy
With a beautiful journey

I look up to the sky
And make the wish of a life
Fulfilled and complete where
Darkness is turned into bright light

Unique and afraid
with so much grace

Challenges created
and finally accepted

REVELATION

Enlightenment awareness
Consciousness awakened
A new dimension
A path created

Gifts of life
For all to bare
Creation of ego and self
Without despair

Meditation frustration
Can be resolved in one
Mind be rested
Actions be tested

Challenges created
And finally accepted
For the journey
To move on

Scenarios repeated are all the same
To further your knowledge and to elevate
Lessons must be learned for you to be
Content fulfilled and full of glee

For those who strive for vitality and life

SUNFLOWER

I'm uncomfortably tall you see
Abundant and almost omnipresent
A combination of black and yellow
The bees embrace my presence

A pale wild perennial in nature
Gorgeously towering over others
Big sequined is my head
A creation of earth mother

Rough serrated upon touch
Sturdy round and often branch
Foundational strength is present
To withstand an avalanche

Petals set in actinomorphic arrangement
Radially symmetric and sterile
Elongated sunlike petal shapes
This is my apparel

Vibrant splendid sun glow
Radiate hope and love
For those who strive for
Vitality energy and life

I'm not just a sunflower you see
For those who are drawn to me
Unwavering faith and unconditional love
I thee to those who inspire to be free

NESHAMA

Spiritual growth   elevate your soul

The spiritual being
A soul bound
In physical form
To enable us to learn

The lessons in life
The journey we have chosen
Is difficult to understand
Ugh! A feeling so broken

Pause for a minute
When you feel lost
Restrain the judgment
Look inside your soul

The answers are at the core
Difficult to see
Will shine like a light
Open up and be free

The confusion is real
Frustration mounted
How do you know
The direction to turn

Free of bias judgment and fear
The fog will disappear
Clarity and focus appear
The direction will be clear

The road is not simple
Although it can be
We make it complex
It doesn't have to be

Breathe in and breathe out
The energy will flow
To bring you back
Back to the core

Spiritual growth
The lessons to learn
To elevate your soul
Is the reason after all

Oh how I miss you
I can't even say

GOODBYE IS NOT FOREVER

The presence of you is gone
But the sound of your voice still echoes on
The pain I feel won't go away
Oh how I miss you I can't even say

Since you parted you always stayed
Close to me in so many ways
Comforting me with words of wisdom
Your guiding light my support system

Last night you appeared- to say goodbye
We hugged for a while and we both cried
You whispered so gently right in my ear
"I love you " you said- your voice was clear

The emptiness you left can't be replaced
By the salty tears gliding slowly down my face
No one knows the longing I feel for you
No one can ever replace you

Goodbye my dearest and a good voyage to you
I know you are close and you hear me too
Our journey together will continue to be
Rooted in the beauty of eternity

The memories we share
how sweet they are

SISTERHOOD

And just like that
Our eyes have met
A friendship started
A family made

We were children then
Learning life's lessons
We're grown today
Really such a blessing

Together we made
Beautiful children
Raised them along
Worth more than a zillion

I remember someone said
Our friendships won't last
It will be short lived
She was wrong and I'm glad

Our soul sisterhood
Began with a few
It needed to grow
add energy to the fuel

The memories we share
How sweet they are
Will continue to etch
With support and love

It's written in the stars
Our journey here
Walk along the path
Of so much to be

Happy big birthday to you
How time flies
I wish you so much
With love in my heart

The chosen path
Depends on you

YOU'RE THE ONE

Negative thoughts
Implanted in your mind
Stemming from the fact
That Super ego is behind

How difficult it is
For you to see
You are destined
To be free

Circumstances arise
For you to be wise
To finally grow
Look deeply into your eyes

The chosen path
Depends on you
To be prudent and astute
Inhale the truth

Reflect before you speak
Breathe in and pause
Calm your mind
Exhale with force

Protected by the light
Darkness purged
A beautiful life
Will finally emerge

You are blessed to be
Awakened to see
A blissful journey can be
Because you hold the key

On the beach

TRANQUILITY

On the beach

Tuesday night
8 O'clock
The summer sun settles down

SILENCE:
Except for the lapping of the waves
As they come closer and closer to me
The gentle breeze touches my face
The smell of fresh air and salty water fills the air
PEACEFULNESS envelops me

Spirit to evolve
through the masters of the world

PRAYER OF THANKS

Time goes by
Days pass on
The minutes are ticking
A physical phenomenon

I awake up at dawn
And say the prayer of thanks
For waking each morning
And to be blessed

I give thanks before you,
King living and eternal
For you have returned within me my soul
With compassion giving and all

Reflections at night
Give insights to thoughts
To see deeper inside
Negativity fought

Every lesson to be learned
On the journey of this road
Spirit to evolve
Through the masters of the world

The morning sun, a nurturing feeling
is a blanket of warmth, feeding my soul

THE MORNING SUN

The morning sun
Never said
That everyday
Will be so great

The morning sun
Rising each day
Visible to see but
Not always displayed

The morning sun
Gives hope and dream
A glimpse of light
A taste of ice cream

The morning sun
Shining it's rays
Food for the existing
Loving in so many ways

The morning sun
A nurturing feeling
Is a blanket of warmth
Feeding my soul

The morning sun
Reminding me each day
To be strong and resilient
Despite of it all

I am the girl
you always think of

I AM

I am the girl you always think of
Silent
Mysterious
Is my game
I make you love me
For what
I am not
The girl you think
I am
Wild
Open
I am all in
DISGUISE

There's the fear of growing up and of the future

GROWING UP

When I look in
The mirror I
See a face
The face of
A girl
An innocent girl
With shame and fear
Respect and
Shyness but
As I look deep
Into her eyes
I see what
No one else sees
There's the
FEAR
Of growing up and of the
FUTURE

Imagine a life
Beautiful and free

BUTTERFLY

Imagine a life
Beautiful and free
A caterpillar once
A butterfly to be

Prisoned by a cocoon
Sealed and protected
Growing inside
A butterfly manifested

Challenges presented
In human form
Ascend through the journey
Your soul transformed

Delicate wings slowly soaring
Penetrating through
And silently roaring

Set your mind with intention
Evolution in the making
Spread your beautiful wings
And reach your potential

Your legacy remains within your heirs
Rest In Peace while you are there

SHARON DEAREST

A breath to breathe in and out
The rising chest a sign of life
Hold on my dear and don't give up
Another day another night

Another day another night
Sun rises at dawn and settles tonight
The night is long and full of hope
Quickly declining like a sharp slope

My head is spinning round and round
The pressors infusing to keep the pressure on
Your soul is moving to new dimensions
Wait it's too fast and beyond comprehension

The ground is dark and very bare
Remember you I will with every prayer
Your legacy remains within your heirs
Rest In Peace while you are there

HE SAID

You had passed just six months ago
Moved on to be in your true home
Greeted by loved ones on the other side
Your essence purified by the bright light

My mind paused since the day you left
The meaning of time still as the surface of a lake
Your presence feels as if it was ages ago
Although I miss you- I did let go

At times when I feel broken
You come and whisper so very softly
I feel your energy message and love
Your guidance brings clarity as you hover above

Time passes by and with each ticking day
I call your name
As I tune your way
Engraved in my hall of fame

I give thanks to you and grateful for your love
Time doesn't heal and the scars just thicken up
They are there for a reason
Your legacy to be remembered

With each passing season

Practice affection and reflection
because rejection is redirection

Purpose

The love we had will
Never go away
HE SAID

The love we share will
Be cherished forever
HE SAID

The love between us
Is so strong and tight
HE SAID.

And one day
Love faded
AND HE WENT AWAY

*The love we had will
never go away, he said*

Your message was clear
Soft spoken and calm
Harsh words uttered
But I didn't mind

Intentions masked by smiles
Cutting tentacles one by one
You were patiently waiting
Devising a plan at the same time

As days went by
You pretended to be
Caring and compassionate
A stinging Bee

To say what you say
Without any meaning
A picture of you emerging
That is not very pretty

You are not who you are
Portraying to others
Self centered inside
Success is all that matters

To be at the top
Feared and respected
But not out of love
It's not so relevant

The stage is yours
That's how you want it to be
Threatened by others
Who dare to see

To think is not allowed
Independence forbidden
You take out the chopping block
It's part of your vision

Nothing lasts forever
And neither will this
Roles get reversed
For you to feel this

*Roles get reversed
for you to feel this*